Published in 2023 by Enslow Publishing, LLC
29 East 21st Street, New York, NY 10010

© 2022 Booklife Publishing
This edition is published by arrangement with
Booklife Publishing

Edited by:
Madeline Tyler

Designed by:
Drue Rintoul

Cataloging-in-Publication Data

Names: Twiddy, Robin.
Title: Upcycling and recycling / Robin Twiddy.
Description: New York : Enslow Publishing, 2023. | Series: Small steps to save the world | Includes glossary and index.
Identifiers: ISBN 9781978530423 (pbk.) | ISBN 9781978530447 (library bound) | ISBN 9781978530430 (6 pack) | ISBN 9781978530454 (ebook)
Subjects: LCSH: Recycling (Waste, etc.)--Juvenile literature. | Sustainable living--Juvenile literature.
Classification: LCC TD794.5 T954 2023 | DDC 363.72'82--dc23

Manufactured in the United States of America

CPSIA compliance information: Batch #CSENS23: For further information contact Enslow Publishing LLC, New York, New York at 1-800-398-2504

Please visit our website, www.enslowpublishing.com. For a free color catalog of all our high-quality books, call toll free 1-800-398-2504 or fax 1-877-980-4454.

Find us on

CONTENTS

Words that look like this are explained in the glossary on page 31.

You can (help) Save the World

The world is in trouble and it needs your help! It needs everyone's help. No one can save the world on their own, but together we can make a change. Our planet is facing many challenges, and lots of these are because of humans. The climate crisis is a big problem. We can see how humans have made it worse by looking at changes in the weather, the oceans, and the air we breathe.

AIR UNSAFE TO BREATHE!

AAAAAAAA AAAAARRRR RGHHH!

TRAFFIC FUMES FILL THE AIR!

PLASTIC FILLS THE OCEANS!

FACTORIES CHOKE THE SKY!

SLUDGE FROM FACTORIES POURS INTO THE OCEAN!

WILDLIFE IS HURT!

THE SMALL STEPS REVOLUTIONARIES

Formed to save the world, the Small Steps Revolution gains new members every day!

Watch with amazement as the Small Steps Revolutionaries save the world one small step at a time!

Featuring Morrison – the Upcycling and Recycling revolutionary!

These are the Small Steps Revolutionaries. They are changing the world one step at a time. Whether it's being energy efficient or learning how to compost, eating locally or living zero waste, recycling or using water wisely, no problem is too big or too small for this band of heroes. By the time you finish this book, you too will be a member of the Small Steps Revolution. Strap in – it's time to save the world!

The first step to becoming a Small Steps Revolutionary is growing your knowledge. This means learning as much as you can about the change you want to see. There are lots of ways to grow your knowledge. Here are some places to get started.

Visit the library — ask the librarian to help you find books about the <u>environment</u> and recycling.

Learn from others — do you know anyone who upcycles? Ask them about it.

Check your local council's website to find out about recycling in your area.

"Knowledge is power — arm yourself!"

"There will not be a magic day when we wake up and it's now OK to express ourselves publicly. We make that day by doing things publicly until it's simply the way things are."
— Tammy Baldwin

Tammy Baldwin is a U.S. <u>senator</u>.

Margaret Fuller was a writer and women's <u>activist</u>. She helped change how people thought about women and their place in the world.

"If you have knowledge, let others light their candles in it." — Margaret Fuller

"Knowledge is of no <u>value</u> unless you put it into practice." – Anton Chekhov

Anton Chekhov wrote plays and short stories that challenged people to think about how they lived.

Research online – there are lots of great websites about upcycling and recycling.

Use an online <u>carbon dioxide</u> (CO_2) calculator to find out what your carbon footprint is. (Your carbon footprint is the amount of CO_2 you make by doing normal, everyday things.)

SMALL STEP: GROW YOUR KNOWLEDGE!

Knowledge is important, but make sure that the information you look at is accurate. A good way to do that is to see who else agrees, writes or talks about the same information. Has it come from a <u>reliable</u> place or person?

Turn the Old into New!

Morrison is a Small Steps Revolutionary. Being a Small Steps Revolutionary means making small changes in your own life to help make a <u>global</u> change and inspire others to do the same.

I don't let anything go to waste. If something is old or broken, I find a new use for it. I do that by recycling and upcycling things. I will explain what that means soon. Recycling and upcycling all of your waste can be hard, so it is best to start with **Small Steps**.

I became a **Small Steps Revolutionary** because there is already way too much garbage in the world, and I wanted to do something about it!

Do you ever wonder what happens to the trash we throw out? A lot of it goes into landfills. Landfill sites are areas where we bury rubbish and waste.

That's disgusting. Sending trash to landfills is the worst way to get rid of our waste. I am going to show you lots of different things to do with your waste that will be better for the environment than sending it to landfills.

It is important that we all try to make less waste. One of the best ways to do this is by recycling and upcycling.

Recycling and Upcycling
– What's the Difference?

You are probably wondering what the difference is between upcycling and recycling. It is important to know how they are different, so let's explore them together.

It all comes down to <u>value</u>. Is your waste becoming something of more value or something of the same value? We can call these upcycling and recycling.

VALUE

RECYCLING – THE SAME OR LESS VALUE

UPCYCLING – MORE VALUE

RECYCLING

Some materials that are recycled are paper, metal, and plastic.

Recycling is when something is broken down and the materials from it are used to make new things such as cans, bottles, and paper. When we recycle, things often get turned into the same thing they were before, such as bottles being used to make more bottles, cardboard used to make more cardboard, and metal from cans used to make new cans.

UPCYCLING

When something is upcycled, it doesn't get broken down into its materials and made into the same thing again. Upcycled things are used in a new way or added to something to make something new.

These are upcycled shoes, given new lives in the garden.

This plastic bottle has been upcycled into a bird feeder.

These bags have been made from old plastic.

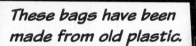

Anything can be upcycled. It just takes some imagination. Even some companies upcycle, taking material that would usually be thrown away and using it to make something new.

SMALL STEPS:
· LEARN THE DIFFERENCE BETWEEN UPCYCLING AND RECYCLING
· UPCYCLE
· RECYCLE

Why Recycle?

It is important that we stop sending our waste to landfills. People have been doing it for years, but it is very bad for the environment. Maybe the generations before us didn't know better, but knowledge isn't just power – it's responsibility.

TOO MANY REASONS TO NAME

- A lot of what goes to landfills is material that could be reused.

- Reusing materials saves the energy needed to make new ones.

- Plastic doesn't biodegrade. When we send plastic to landfills, it can sit there for hundreds of years.

- Even when plastic does break down, it breaks into smaller pieces of plastic that damage the soil and water.

GREENHOUSE GASES

Food, cardboard, wood, and cloth are all examples of <u>organic waste</u>. When organic waste breaks down, it releases greenhouse gases. These gases are a big part of the climate crisis. If we can stop sending so much waste to landfills by recycling more, we will have taken one BIG step toward saving the world.

SOIL AND WATER POLLUTION

<u>Chemicals</u> and <u>toxins</u> seep into the ground at landfill sites and make the soil dangerous for animals and plants to live in. These same chemicals get into water too. This harms wildlife and affects the plants that grow in these areas.

As Small Steps Revolutionaries, it is our responsibility to do what we can to send less waste to landfills.

The Story of a Can

Billy and his friends are hanging out and having fun. Billy has a can of soda. It's his favorite.

Billy has finished his drink and is now faced with a dilemma! Which bin should he put his can in?

Billy chooses to throw his can into the general waste bin.

The general waste bin — including Billy's empty can — is collected.

The general waste is taken to a landfill site where the truck unloads the waste.

Billy made a poor choice putting his can in the general waste. Billy's can will sit in the landfill site for between 80 and 200 years before it biodegrades.

Look, it's Billy's can!

Let's see what would have happened if Billy had taken the **Small Step** of putting his can in the right bin.

So, faithful reader, we return to young Billy as he is faced with his dilemma again. Which bin, Billy?

Billy makes the right choice and puts his empty can in the recycling bin.

The recycling is collected.

It arrives at the recycling center, where the recycling is sorted. Billy's can is separated with the other cans.

The cans are washed, then crushed together.

The crushed cans are melted down and used to make new cans.

The new cans are delivered to stores.

Those new cans wait on the shelves to be bought again.

Thanks to Billy taking a Small Step and making the right choice, his old can has been made into lots of new cans!

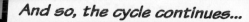

And so, the cycle continues...

Upcycle It!

Upcycling is all about being creative: looking at something old or worn-out and imagining what else could be done with it. Upcycling is about turning trash into treasure.

I am going to show you some upcycling ideas you can try at home. Hopefully this will inspire you to get creative and come up with some ideas of your own.

SCRAP NOTEBOOK

Do your grown-ups get lots of letters? Instead of putting the envelopes they come in into the recycling, why not upcycle them and make your own scrap notebook!

1. Get all of your envelopes together.

2. Cut them into the same-sized rectangles.

3. Fold them in the middle to make a book.

4. Take a piece of cardboard (maybe from a cereal box or a delivery) and cut it to the same size as the envelope rectangles.

5. Fold this around the outside of your paper book – this is the cover.

6. Now staple your book in the middle.

7. You can use stickers or pictures from magazines to decorate it.

UPSEWING

If you can sew, you will never need to throw out old clothes again. Being able to sew doesn't just mean you can fix clothes — it also means you can turn old clothes into something new.

I turned these old jeans into a bag.

OLD TENNIS BALLS INTO NEW HELPERS

Upcycling can be fun and <u>functional</u>. Let's turn these old tennis balls into something useful. A few dots from a marker and a cut for a mouth will turn an old tennis ball into a funky little guy. When you squeeze the sides, its mouth opens and you can store things inside!

Buy to Recycle

As a **Small Steps Revolutionary**, one of the steps that I take is to make sure that the things I buy can be recycled. I do this by looking at what materials the things I buy are made from. You should always make sure to check what the packaging is made from, too!

You've got to think about what you buy!

PLASTIC

METAL

CARDBOARD

PAPER AND CARDBOARD

If I have a choice between something wrapped in plastic or packaged in cardboard and paper, I will always try to buy things covered in paper and cardboard because I know these can be recycled. Remember, not all plastic can be recycled.

Which one should I buy?

This one because it is reusable and recyclable.

Metal bottles are better than plastic bottles because they can be reused.

PLASTIC

There are many plastics that can be recycled. Some countries use symbols to tell you what type of plastic something is made from and if it can be recycled. When you buy something, check to see if it has a recycling symbol on it. If it can be recycled, check what types of plastics your local recycling accepts.

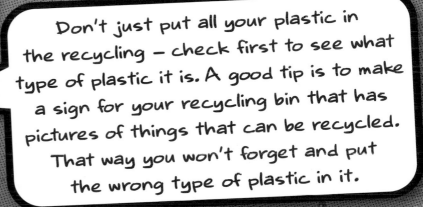

Don't just put all your plastic in the recycling — check first to see what type of plastic it is. A good tip is to make a sign for your recycling bin that has pictures of things that can be recycled. That way you won't forget and put the wrong type of plastic in it.

These things can usually be recycled:

DRINK BOTTLES

GLASS BOTTLES

PLASTIC BOTTLES

DRINK CANS

FOOD CANS

EGG CARTONS

SMALL STEPS:
- BUY THINGS THAT COME IN RECYCLABLE PACKAGING
- MAKE A SIGN WITH THE TYPES OF PLASTICS YOU CAN RECYCLE ON IT

Upcycled Art

TURN YOUR WASTE INTO WORKS OF ART

There are lots of ways to upcycle, but one of my favorite ways is through art. I save up all the waste that I can't recycle or repurpose and use it to make art. As with all upcycling, it is all about being imaginative and creative.

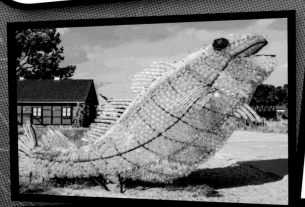

THE POWER OF ART

Activists have always used art to spread their messages. As a Small Steps Revolutionary, you can do the same. Check out some of this powerful art from <u>environmentalists</u> around the world.

Making animals out of trash is a powerful way of telling the world about how waste is bad for wildlife.

You can use old candy wrappers, bottle lids, snack bags and more to make art with a message. Just use your imagination, and make sure that the waste you use is clean before you start.

You can use your waste to make a <u>collage</u> picture, or even a <u>sculpture</u>.

I made this turtle from green plastic waste to raise awareness about how plastic harms sea turtles' habitats. What environmental message is important to you? What kind of art could you make to share your message?

What do you do with your old clothes? Don't throw them away! There are lots of things that you can do with old clothes.

REPURPOSE

Old T-shirts make great cleaning rags. Cut them up and reuse them!

MEND

The first thing to think about is whether your clothes can be mended. If you or someone you know can sew, you might be able to save that favorite sweater or pair of jeans. Patches are a great way to fix holes.

DONATE

If your clothes are just too small or you don't like wearing them anymore, think about <u>donating</u> or selling them. Someone else could still enjoy them.

SMALL STEPS FASHION

You can take **Small Steps** when you buy clothes. Secondhand clothes can be found at markets and charity stores all over the place. If you look carefully, you can find some really cool and unusual clothes!

There are even **Small Steps Revolutionaries** working in the fashion industry. Lots of clothes makers are using recycled materials in their clothes. Check the labels on clothes to see if they are made with any recycled materials.

SMALL STEPS:
- MEND
- REPURPOSE
- DONATE
- BUY SECONDHAND

Believe it or not, some clothes are even made from recycled plastic bottles!

Surprising Recycling

SURPRISINGLY RECYCLABLE

There are lots of things that can be recycled that might surprise you.

There are places that recycle crayons – they can even be turned into new crayons!

Some stores collect old running shoes to recycle. Search online to see if there is somewhere you can get rid of your old sneakers.

Many local recycling centers recycle old string lights.

Ask your optician if they collect old glasses. Your glasses can go to other people who need them.

There are many charities that take old mobile phones. They raise money by fixing them and selling them to stores. You can also take them to your local recycling center, where they will take out the useful electronic parts to be reused.

There are lots of things that you would think aren't recyclable that are, and others that you might think you could put in your regular recycling bin at home that you shouldn't.

Polystyrene cannot be recycled like other materials. You should not put it in your recycling bin.

Plastic bags can't be recycled in your recycling bin at home. There are some places that you can take plastic bags where they can be made into new things.

When paper gets wet, the fibers that it is made of get broken down, which makes it impossible to recycle.

Even though wet wipes are made from paper, they can't be recycled. They should never be put in the recycling bin.

Pizza boxes absorb too much grease and food to be recycled. You can put them in your compost bin or compost pile if you break them into small pieces.

25

Become a Champion of Change

Being a Small Steps Revolutionary is more than just the Small Steps you take — it's about spreading the message and helping others take their first Small Steps. We can do this by sharing our own Small Steps.

RAISING AWARENESS

There are lots of ways that you can raise awareness as a Small Steps Revolutionary. Some revolutionaries use social media to share their message. Recruit an adult to help you manage an account. Remember not to use social media without an adult you trust.

SPEAK WITH YOUR ART

If you are creative, you could make some art from waste just like on page 20. Use your art to help spread the upcycling and recycling message.

Share your creations online with #smallstepsrevolution

HELP WHERE YOU CAN

Be the change you want to see.

Look for places that you can make a change. Are there any Small Steps you could help a family member to make? Maybe you could help your grandparents, aunts, uncles, or cousins take some of the Small Steps in this book.

I helped my aunt with what she can and can't put in the recycling bin.

Small Steps Revolutionaries are proud to make a change!

Share your successes with the hashtag #smallstepsrevolution

Remember, it is important to spread awareness about recycling and upcycling, but not everyone understands why it is important. People are more likely to try to make a change themselves if you are helpful instead of being mean to them – this is the Small Steps way!

SMALL STEP: SPREAD YOUR MESSAGE

Ethical Living

Recycling and upcycling is only one part of the Small Steps Revolution, so what does it mean to be a Small Steps Revolutionary? It means living ethically – living the best life you can. To live ethically, you need to think about the effect your actions have on the world around you.

MAKING THE CHANGE

Changing the way we live is hard. Make sure that you make small, manageable changes and stick to them. Remember the golden rule: Small Steps Lead to Big Change.

A good way to guide your actions as a Small Steps Revolutionary is to live by the Five Rs. They are:

REFUSE – BEFORE YOU BUY SOMETHING, THINK HARD ABOUT WHETHER YOU NEED IT OR NOT. IF YOU DON'T, THEN REFUSE TO BUY OR ACCEPT IT.

REDUCE – SOME THINGS YOU WILL NOT BE ABLE TO REFUSE, BUT YOU CAN USE LESS. THIS WILL MEAN YOU CREATE LESS WASTE.

REUSE – BEFORE YOU THROW SOMETHING AWAY, THINK ABOUT WHETHER THAT THING CAN BE USED AGAIN. ONLY REPLACE SOMETHING IF IT CAN'T BE USED AGAIN.

REPURPOSE – THIS IS ANOTHER WAY OF SAYING UPCYCLE. IF YOU CAN, FIND A NEW WAY TO USE SOMETHING INSTEAD OF THROWING IT AWAY.

RECYCLE – IF YOU CAN'T DO ANY OF THESE THINGS, THEN YOU SHOULD TRY TO RECYCLE. MAKE SURE THAT WHAT YOU PUT INTO YOUR RECYCLING BIN CAN BE RECYCLED BY YOUR LOCAL RECYCLING CENTER.

Manifesto

THE UPCYCLING AND RECYCLING MANIFESTO

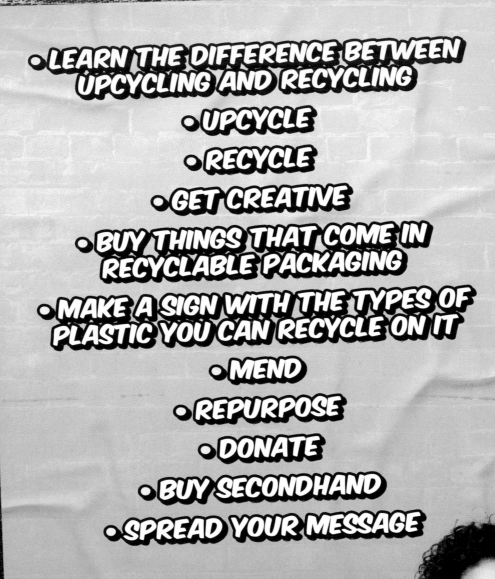

- LEARN THE DIFFERENCE BETWEEN UPCYCLING AND RECYCLING
- UPCYCLE
- RECYCLE
- GET CREATIVE
- BUY THINGS THAT COME IN RECYCLABLE PACKAGING
- MAKE A SIGN WITH THE TYPES OF PLASTIC YOU CAN RECYCLE ON IT
- MEND
- REPURPOSE
- DONATE
- BUY SECONDHAND
- SPREAD YOUR MESSAGE

You are now a full member of the **Small Steps Revolution**. Keep on taking small, _sustainable_ steps, spreading the word, and inspiring others to do the same. Together we can and will **Save the World**.

Glossary

ACTIVIST	someone who does things to raise awareness about a cause
BIODEGRADE	to break down due to living things such as bacteria
CARBON DIOXIDE	a natural colorless gas found in air
CHEMICALS	substances that are made or used by scientists
CLIMATE CRISIS	serious problems being caused by changes to the world's weather, caused by humans and the release of greenhouse gases into the environment
COLLAGE	pictures made by putting together lots of pictures
DONATING	giving away for free, usually to a charity
ENVIRONMENT	all of the things that make up the natural world
ENVIRONMENTALISTS	people who work to protect the environment
FIBERS	things that are like threads
FUNCTIONAL	serving a purpose
GENERATIONS	groups of people who lived around the same time
GLOBAL	having to do with the whole world
ORGANIC WASTE	a type of waste that is made up of natural things such as food
POLYSTYRENE	a type of plastic that is often used in packaging
RECRUIT	to bring a member into a group
RELIABLE	can be trusted
RESPONSIBILITY	the need to take on a task or a job that you are trusted to and should do
SCULPTURE	a statue made by an artist
SENATOR	someone who helps run a country as a member of part of the government
SUSTAINABLE	able to be used without damaging future generations
TOXINS	poisonous things
VALUE	what something is worth

Index